That Special Something

That Special Something

poems

John Popielaski

Sheila-Na-Gig Editions

ISBN: 978-1-962405-21-8
Library of Congress Control Number: 2025937252

Sheila-Na-Gig Editions
Russell, KY
Hayley Mitchell Haugen, Editor
www.sheilanagigblog.com

Acknowledgments

The author gratefully acknowledges the editors of the following publications, where these poems first appeared:

Bluestem: "Unnecessary Harm"
Broadkill Review: "Leaving the Oldest Tree in Maine Alone"
Canary: "Bear Encounter," "Mountain Lion"
Cave Wall: "The Passing On"
Clade Song: "Aesthetics," "Pardon"
Common Ground Review: "Breaking with Tradition," "Drifting from the Faith"
Counterpunch: "Whatever Will Be"
Dark Horse: "Rescue"
Freshwater: "Priming a Flying Rafter Near the End of August"
The Hollins Critic: "Elegy for American Toad"
Home Planet News: "Eighty-Sixed," "Prevailing Winds"
Medicinal Purposes: "Washington Crossing the Delaware"
New South: "How Fragile Is the Peace"
Ontario Review: "Toward Purity"
Poetrybay: "On Not Shooting"
Redivider: "Dive Bar"
Right Hand Pointing: "Accidents of Birth"
Roanoke Review: "Opossums"
Sheila-Na-Gig online: "A Generous Inaction," "Anecdote of Way Northeast of Tennessee," "Vastness and the Theme of Inescapability"
South Dakota Review: "After Saint Eustace"
Sterling: "On the Virtues of the Unadventurous," "Trapped"
Theodate: "Camped," "Civil Disobedience"
Toad, The Journal: "Novice," "That Special Something"
Tulane Review: "Trespass"
White Whale Review: "Isn't It Romantic?"

Several of these poems previously appeared in the chapbook *Isn't It Romantic?* (Texas Review Press) or in the chapbook *O, Captain* (The Ledge Press).

For Steve Lewis and Andrew Sheldon,

and in memory of Henry Taylor

Contents

"The point of all this was to stay alive
as long as decency required."

—Marilynne Robinson, *Jack*

That Special Something

Waking in a two-person tent
is best if you're one person.
Territorial ambition then
is not an issue.
You can focus
on the filtered light
and argue with yourself
about the singer of the song
you woke to: thrush
one minute, waxwing next.
Unzip, emerge. Release urea
in the designated area,
direct yourself to stream,
and filter water
for the morning. Even here
you never know
what microbe has it out for you.
But even so, you know
this is no pioneer
experience, no death trap,
no frontier, and thus
is not authentic,
not evocative
of your resourcefulness
because your presence here
is mayfly and you'll die
to this life, waking
on the other side
where you will move
from cubicle to cubicle
and sip drip coffee,
fret about such silly things
as thread counts
or the mail

and spend so much
of your allotted time
in front of one screen or another
that you know you are
a poser here. You're not
a black bear or a fiddlehead.
You don't belong.
On one tree is a sign
for north. On one tree
is a sign for south.
Your path is chosen.
It is practically impossible
to get yourself so lost
that you forget what you have left
behind. You fantasize
about rebellion as you roll
your sleeping bag
and you resolve
to sabotage the turbine
for the windmill that's to be
erected on the ridge ahead.
You never will
because you know
subversion isn't in you
and your parents didn't raise you
to give up yourself to something
as granitic as that ridge.

On the Virtues of the Unadventurous

Because I had been taught to love
the hero, he who ventures farther
than the person who's content
to follow up a plough horse
or to sit in peace behind a book
when glory's elsewhere to be won,
it took me years before I wondered
if Columbus had been moral,
if a better man, encountering the natives,
would have honored their existence,
sailing back to Europe, keeping mum.
There is the practical school
that says because it happened
it could not have happened otherwise.
There is the school that's willing
to admit a slight revision, arguing
that someone else, a like mind
with a monarch's backing,
would have come along regardless
and begun the westward decimation,
ending with the albatross,
the sailor's friend, ingesting plastic
floating like synthetic krill
in the Pacific Ocean,
which Balboa spotted from a mountaintop
and claimed as property of Spain.

Washington Crossing the Delaware

As confident as Washington appears to be,
his black boot planted on the gunwale
of the modest boat his men row through the ice,
he had no prophet to consult before embarking,
no one who could summarize the secret future,
sparing him some guesswork in a war
as monumental as the one that ruined Troy.

Bobbing on the Delaware, as stoic as a gull,
he does not seem to think at all
about the sea-borne Greeks, who knew
the first to disembark from their impressive fleet
would be the first to feel a glorious spear
impale him on a Trojan beach.

He knows that soldiers snooze in Trenton,
prayed for by their foreign mothers
who so missed their boys this Christmas,
no one like Laocoon to warn their sons
of danger, no one like Cassandra,
burdened cruelly by awareness,
to avert their doom if they would heed her.

James Monroe is struggling with the flag
but peering in the same direction
as his focused general, who might crack
a smile if he knew that only two
of his two-thousand men will die this morning,
shivering and blue, hypothermic victims
of a mid-Atlantic cold front
and inadequate shoes.

The Orbital, The Globular, and The Linear

"I'm just glad to be here, happy to be alive."
—The Traveling Wilburys, "End of the Line"

It's nice to think a squirrel could have made it
in the old days all the way from the Atlantic Ocean
to the Mississippi River, tree to tree
to tree, a shiver through what would have seemed
like endless canopy, a perfectly adherent
airborne density that not a single time
would have come down for passage on the ground.

This is the sort of thing some people think about
when they declare this is the year they'll finally hike
the Appalachian Trail and never make it
to the trailhead where the people they would like to be
wait season after season for a sign of their arrival.

It's the sort of thing some people who would like to live
their parceled lives according to the principles of something
like harmonious non-interference think about
in late spring as they lean back at reposeful angles
in their cedar chairs and watch a modern squirrel
leap from beech to beech to maple after maple, dipping
with each gripped branch and recovering,
no fear of plummeting and probably no wondering if,
of all the ways, this should have been the one.

The few who still experience the phantom pangs
when they imagine what the forest used to be
take solace in the massive sugar maple
whose circumference whispers that the tree was here
before the Revolution, but they know
the measurement and calculation don't change
any of the things that have to change or else.

Some know the Tao does not take sides,
but some wish that it would. Some understand
the Tao more deeply and give up
their houses and their cars and look askance
at their employments, which made possible the stellar
payment histories that entities
that charged for everything except the air
reported to the forces whose imaginary voices
sounded godly when they said their credit scores were high.

Some climb the dawn walls after quitting.
Some walk far and wrestle with their consciences
as they bum rides to get them closer
to the jungles of Peru or to the tundra.
Some do hike the long trails. Some tiptoe
to the last few truly silent places
and lie down when they arrive, examining
the clouds, which even there are not unknown
to take the shapes of warships, aircraft
carriers, merchant vessels flying
the insignia, signs that in the halls of power down below
a chorus rises, warning of the possibility
of nautical aggression flaring in the Arctic
Ocean, telling us to picture possibly
perpetual supply-chain interruptions,
asking us how would we feel if we,
the seventeenth or so most free,
were always threatened like the sitting duck
that is Taiwan, concluding that the world
is less pacific, possibly, than it has ever been,
concluding, necks craned, that it's vital
to project more force than our misguided
enemies onto the ever-neutral sea.

Civil Disobedience

I've plotted to go out at night
and drive spikes into trees
to thwart the long-barred chainsaws
and to make the lumberjack
who never felt quite right in goggles
lose an eye and wish he'd never
taken up this line of work,
but my conviction fades when I imagine
reading Edward Abbey novels
hour after hour in a jail cell
that I only leave for meals
and to improve for martial purposes
my scholarly physique.
At times I picture Gandhi walking,
and I feel it's okay to believe
a violent path is not for me.
I think it is much better to become
like Julia Hill and climb a redwood,
live for two years on a bough
while lumber-company executives
confer with lawyers in a paneled room
and dance around the moral thing to do.

Novice

I bought a little land on which to practice
living three or four weeks at a time
without electric power, to accept
some limitations and be nothing
but a point of light in darkness,
vanishing when what I needed
light for had been done. There is no
difference, I suppose. Beholden
to incinerated coal
or alkaline is nonetheless
beholden. Go back farther
and rely on firelight not generated
by a lighter or a match
and you are closer to escaping
the contemporary tendency
to charge you with pretending
to be someone you are not.
I'm still dependent on the match,
but, in the absence of a tap,
I take my buckets to the brook
and lay them in a pool
where small trout congregate
beneath the water striders
who defy the downstream pull.
Acquaintances who've visited
suggest I dam the way
and use a pump and generator
for the uptake to eliminate
the slight barbarity
of going *to* the water
as opposed to making it
shift course and come to me.
I nod and do not bother
to explain I want to simplify
or understand up close at least

how infrastructure blots out
something elemental in our lives
and distances necessity,
grants too much ease.

Camped

No mirror here to document the growth
of whiskers, to delineate
the geographical encroachment
of the hairline and the laugh lines
into regions they had never crept before.
What evidence there is of an auteur
is muted by the ear's attention
to the song of stream and wood thrush,
by the eye's unreasoning
appreciation of the hula dance
the tallest hemlock does.
My friend is wreathed in pipe smoke,
contemplating probably
the secrets of the speed square,
how we had today discovered
that a point inscribed at a particular degree,
a pivot of the speed square, and a line drawn
at that angle will declare
what pitch the cabin's roof will be.
Pythagoras, though, is interesting
more for his sincere believing
in the transmigration of the soul,
for his believing that he heard
his dead friend's voice one evening
in a dog's bark, something I have tried
to do without success so far as one by one
the beings I am closest to die off and leave
so little of themselves to cross.

Priming a Flying Rafter Near the End of August

A wrinkled lip in sympathy
means nothing to the butterfly
who touched down briefly
in the quart-sized can
of primer that I held
as guardedly as one can
in the middle of the woods
where no one in my tribe
would hear me fall.
I clamp my yellow teeth down
on the speckled handle
of the paintbrush
and descend, regretting
how the civilized collide
so easily and often
with the wild.
What remedy I have to offer
makes descending sillier
than staying on the ladder,
brushstroke after brushstroke,
until the fluttering subsides
and the first beer of the evening
beckons, promising
to do a little something
with the sorrow that sobriety
refuses to assuage.

After Saint Eustace

Shouldering a sack of cracked corn
through a dervish cloud of gnats,
the lifting of the day's heat an occasion
to be celebrated with commotion,
I take two rock steps to the underbrush
that fortifies the hill the deer come down
like spirits in the evening, wary
of the one or two lights in the ranch house
I will next year side with cedar.

I slit the corn sack with my pocketknife
and recall Durer's engraving,
the one with five hounds wondering
why they have been called off, the stag,
a little smug, so close that they can taste him,
their master off his horse and kneeling
on the margin of the woods, his sword
and dagger sheathed, no bow or quiver
to be seen, as meek as any runt.

Meekness was the first step in accepting
that the crucifix on the buck's head
was not some rustic's notion of a joke
to trick a noble into false belief,
to make him ride back to the castle
on the mountain in the background
and convince the smirking skeptics, living
in the twilight of the Roman gods,
that Christ addressed him in the woods.

The corn cache hidden in the dwindling
green, I stand behind the kitchen
window, lights off, glasses on, attempting
to discern a white tail or an antler
moving toward my offering, the tree frogs

starting up the "All is well"
as if to tell the muted animals
it's safe now to come out, the man
appears to have retired for the night.

Elegy for American Toad

Forties last night. August wanes.
Not long before the toads go under.

I have spent the summer treading lightly,
almost tiptoe, on the tall grass,
toad-mined. Failed once.
Viscera. You get the picture.

Closure sometimes is a grave.

I dug one, lined it seriously
with fringe grass, lowered him
by one leg, more grass, soil,
capstone, no inscription.

Sometimes it is not.

Night. Clay pipe like a firefly.
No mating calls. I wonder
if the bad news made the rounds.

A garter snake slides by,
a shadow in the window light.
Coyotes somewhere.

Cold.

How Fragile Is the Peace

If somehow I have managed
to focus my philanthropy
on creatures that get stepped on,
shot at, struck by someone
speeding to the package store
before it closes with a sign flip
for the night, which draws
the deer down to the yard's edge
where I pile cracked corn
like a traitor to a cause
my kind has championed
as necessary for the good,
I do not mean to seem unneighborly.
I wave before I'm waved to,
and I only use the chainsaw
to make cordwood after leaves flare
in what light is left these afternoons,
although there is an ordinance
that says we're not allowed
to leave out food for animals
we do not formally tend,
and this I have ignored
with an insurgent regularity,
which bothers Henry, I suspect,
although he has not hailed me over
to the shrub- and pine-lined boundary
where such matters in the past
have had their airing
in the small talk that we speak,
like diplomats, in code, aware
how fragile is the peace.

Trapped

Len is in his sixties and adjusting
to the surgery that raised his stomach
to a place that isn't natural.
For a while, it was weep and woe,
the mind preparing for the trip across.
He has a hundred-sixty acres, which he sees
are his an eyeblink, raising in his mind
the question of just who owns whom.
He has begun to put specific prices
on his guns so that his wife will know
the market prices when the time comes.
He feels a little better, good enough
to walk the property and set the leg traps.
In November at a gathering, he passes
out the photos of a fox, a bobcat,
a few coyotes, wide-eyed, one leg
ambushed by the sprung contraptions.
Pocketing his camera, he approached
each one with steadied pistol,
indicating with his eyes no mercy, feeling
in control of something in the world
he sensed would not be his for long.

The Passing On

So a father dies before his son
can prove the years of boozing were a phase,
an interim whose sorrow was supposed
to make the son's eventual return
sufficient restitution for his fall.

A sigh.

And here is the return: the son,
established on this acre now,
is in the middle of his second month
of studying the cedar shingles
that he spirit levels twice and nails
twice, rusticating gradually
this house his father never knew.

Loss sometimes taps him on the shoulder
when he's not expecting and suggests
he take a moment to consider
for the millionth time the soul
and its mysterious departure
from the body he remembers
for its peasant's tan, its crooked nose,
its thick, industrious hands.

And he considers how so many
overemphasize the dumb improvement
of succeeding generations
in a more or less financial sense
and often overlook the passing on
of skills that don't advance the family honor much
but lift the dipped line just enough
so straightness is what registers
with those who push the strollers by.

Strange

The other day I did a thing I'm certain
that my father never thought to do.
I spent a quarter of my paycheck
on an oil painting by a friend
I haven't seen in more than twenty years.
It's sixteen by twenty inches,
and I wonder where I got the gene
that has no problem with me staring
at the space I have allotted for the painting
on the wall between the living room and kitchen.
Like my father, I had not considered
how much time is necessary
for such art to fully dry.
So I'll be driving to my friend's house
near the Hudson River at the end
of May to claim the painting,
which is called *Strange House*,
and do a little hiking in the Catskills,
which I'm certain is another thing
my father never thought to do.
As you can probably tell, I'm trying,
since it's been so long,
to hold more tightly to my father,
to remember similarities
and differences as clearly as I can.
When times were tight,
I went with my father to his night job
cleaning banks. We vacuumed,
dumped the trash cans, stood beside
each other polishing the vault door,
strangers somehow but beloved.

In Praise of Breathing

We take so many breaths,
inevitable, involuntary,
that it mostly feels unlikely
there will ever be a last.
But then one afternoon a mountain
underfoot keeps rising,
or an allergen eludes the cilia
and lodges, or a cancer cell continues
its division in a speckled lung,
and we are forced to wish
that we could go back
to a golden age of breathing.
If we can go back, we hold
what sparrows in our palms we can
and promise to affix
reflective stickers to the windows,
and, when one too many sparrows breathes
its last, we finally affix
the stickers, feeling
we have made a good mark on the world,
and go about attempting to repair
another pang. We end up
sometimes in a graveyard,
staring at a pair of hyphenated dates
and picturing cigar smoke belly dancing
from the mouth and nostrils
of the man the marker names.
On two feet in the sunlight,
we imagine whether anything is left
of his esophagus, his lungs,
his poor alveoli and cilia,
or whether down there in the darkness
is an empty rib cage held together
by the nicest shirt his wife at least
a hundred-fifty-million breaths ago could find.

Dive Bar

I could blame the damned Sumerians
for stumbling on the alchemy
of fermentation, but I won't.

The archaeologists who brushed away
the sediment that scabbed the beer pots
guessed it all began by dropping
bread crumbs into water for a reason
buried somewhere in cuneiform.

Ninkasi, brewing goddess, sung to, smiled,
and the drinking song was born.

This sense of worship filtered down,
moved west and stopped a while
in Ireland before the exploration-
minded fellows sailed a little
farther, fucking with the natives
in what had been quite a stable land.

I don't know when the barstool came
about, but I cannot imagine
anyone developing a better perch
on which to spend a late night
like a ruined owl, numb
to lamentation in suburbia.

Rescue

Today a one-eyed dog was scratching
at the back door in a thunderstorm.
The statue of Saint Francis in the garden
then seemed more than ornamental.
Glad to think of something other
than relentless debt, I let him in
and asked him questions while he cocked his head
as though I might be understood
if only he could find the proper angle.
My wife, the keeper of the towels, dried
his little body, checked his teeth,
determined he was old, and felt
say blessed, say chosen as an agent
of a rescue that may easily have been
assigned to someone less say willing
to accept this type of mission to the end.
Snubbed by He who dictates, *You may have
a child, and you may not*, she's open
to what beings come her way—a litter
of abandoned moles, a fledgling
sparrow, wind-blown, a turtle crossing
a perilous road—and suffers when they pass.

A Matter of Convenience

Each morning I walk down the right side
of a gravel driveway and then up
the left side, which becomes the right, head down
as though each contact lens I've ever known
has popped out and is hiding from me
with a smirk in the vicinity.
Last night's humidity, a gloss, lies on
the gravel, gray as catbirds eye me.
A slug, as gray as gravel, retracts atop
a gravel mesa I relocate to the humus.
I prefer to do such things in secret.
Why, then, do I write them down
and hope for distribution?
The consensus is that slugs are pests
and ought to die for the consensus.
The agriculture college lists four ways
to kill them and does not reflect at all
on undulation or tranquility.
My wife's Toyota's been remotely started
and will be reversing down the driveway shortly.
She has helped some turtles cross the quiet roads,
but that is where she draws a line
as arbitrary as the one so many of us draw
between one animal as foodstuff
and another as beloved pet,
whose loss will be transmuted
by a tale about a rainbow bridge.

Trespass

I try compassion, but the constant wheezing
of my wife is sometimes too much
and I step out of the house
as if I do not plan to enter it again.
This is illusion, I'm aware,
but it is better than my rendering
acceptable a time shift
that permits the first beer to go down
this early in the morning.
I've checked my genealogy
on websites on the off chance
I'm descended from a Polish count
or an industrialist whose money
is collecting dust and only needs my claim
to do some good among the living.
I'm aware this is illusion, too.
Don't let me fool you, though.
There's joy out here and lessons
I believe can be applied to make life
lift me up before I have to go
inside the well-appointed coop again.
I don't know why a chickadee can free me
of the gloominess or why a deer
who doesn't run can make me feel accepted
by the world our settlement crowds out
or why this naked man asleep
beneath my hedge inspires me
to spray him with the garden hose,
why, for the moment, I'm as happy
as I've ever been alone.

Toward Purity

Sitting in the evening at his desk,
the first Victorians not born yet,
Thomas Bowdler expurgates another
Shakespeare play and rolls his eyes
to indicate such genius should have been above
such double meanings and such expletives.

He does not countenance the groundlings,
grinning skeletons in common graves,
who used to hurl their rotten vegetables
at the stage when unamused,
demanding their diversion in the style
they had long since grown accustomed to.

His audience does not weather plague
as often, does not need the theater
quite as dearly for catharsis,
does not crave Elizabethan bawdiness
to mitigate Elizabethan woe,
which ceased two centuries ago.

It wants the rough-hewn edges of the world
smoothed down by men like Bowdler,
perched by well-snuffed candlelight, a scribe
with an agenda, patiently rewriting
what is vulgar in the record, mortified
by how much dirty work there is to do.

Whatever Will Be

Asbestos is a little town
in southeast Canada
where mining is a way
of life and it is impolite
to ask if mesothelioma
or related ailments of the lung
are common or accepted,
part of doing business
with a microscopic fiber
that will not dissolve in water
or consent to alteration via flame.

I am descending
toward the little town,
and I imagine angels down there
batting fibers faithfully away
from the defenseless mouths and noses
of the Quebecois who answer
inquiries about the air
by smiling and reminding
the inquirers we all
must die of something
that we would with white masks
or with forearms
or with wishful thinking
try like hell to shun.

Prevailing Winds

The February meeting of the local chapter
of the Voluntary Human Extinction Movement
was at my house, which was lit a bulb
more brightly than it would have been.

The evening's opening topic was the cloud
of vinyl-chloride vapor murmuring
like starlings toward us from the grave
derailment in East Palestine, Ohio.

Of the four of us, just one had read *White Noise.*
As usual he wore a sable chevron
on each canvas sleeve to prove
his faith in irony was durable.

What action could we have proposed?
We had no powers of dispersion.

Critics say we traffic in despair.
But we ate hummus sprinkled with paprika.
We drank fruity beer.
We did the natural thing. We hoped
the plume would murmur north of us
or murmur south, but such hope was unjust.

Why shouldn't it swirl over us?

We talked about how every species
but this version of our own
cooperated naturally with Earth.

We talked about how we would like to leave
no trace when we pass on,
no progeny to make the same mistakes.

But we will leave behind our rubber
soles, our microplastics, contacts,
circuits, countertops, composites, tires
that will make it through an ice age.

We put our jackets on and went
outside to look up at the sky.
A rich man's string of satellites

outdid the stars, and in the air
the scent of mown hay and chlorine.

Opossums

They are born in a brush pile before the spring's full bloom.
Their embryonic digits grasp. They pull
each blind and hairless fraction of a gram, each portion
of audacity, across the mother to the pouch seam.
Each crawls in, a jostled grain. Each claims a nipple, curls
and fuses, dreams and purrs.

Their mother teaches patience, silence, placement.

Sounds and smells that tense their mother
enter them and leave deep marks. The babies cling more
tightly during tensions. They take refuge in her skin.

Contact matters more than anything.

Day by day, their mother tells the story
of the touched and untouched. She tells it
when she leaves the brush pile in the dark,
her babies fastened in her pouch. She tells it
when she picks up peanuts scattered by a fragrance
on an unlit patio. She tells it
in the budding woods when the coyote scent is strong
and when the flora and mycelia are songs. She tells it
by the river and the river trash. She tells it
in the strawberry fields and pastureland. And in between
these places, as her babies cling, she tells
the story of the land that least forgives, where dead lie
everywhere and are ground down, where light bears down
at unreal speed and all that can be done is to be stunned.

One night, her babies' eyes still weeks away
from opening, she climbs a brownstone monument and perches
on the brownstone kepi of a brownstone Union soldier.

Across the road the soldier overlooks, a house
from settlement times is dark inside. Fine bugs
and moths exhaust themselves beneath a low-glare streetlight.

She rises on her hind legs like a fur hat come to life.

Her babies, tucked away, do not see
what she sees. They do, however, feel the undertow
of the road below. They feel the river's undertow
beyond the field behind the house. They hear
the cables and the wires in the earth and overhead. They hear
the pipeline water underground. They smell
the stew of sewage, smell shed particles of tires, unending butts
of cigarettes, smell leaks and spills, emissions, infinite particulates.

She lies down for a while, forelegs resting
on the kepi's bill. Her babies press against her, touched
by her alone. She tells each one the story only opossums know.
When she is done, she rises on her hind legs once again.
The spirits of the short-lived and resourceful come.
The whiskers of the spirits who lived through
the southern exodus transmit. The spirits of the margins
and humility see signs that the indifferent
and disintegrated will not rule forever. By tradition
and example, the transmissions counsel,
leave a path for those who will come after.

Unnecessary Harm

An act of charity
that is not tax deductible
and is conducted nightly
on the fringes of my yard
is my depositing about ten pounds
of cracked corn for the deer
I have with spectacles regarded
with a convert's ardor
since my late exposure
to Durer's depiction
of a Roman's genuflection
to a ten-point, otherworldly
ruminant he had
with bow pursued through woods.
I know I am contributing
to the inaudible explosion
of the population
of such animals the likes of which
humanity since long before
the advent of the spearhead
or the wheat row would be rid.
So field mice come. So opossums come.
So ticks are carried nigh,
and I remember reading somewhere
Jainists let mosquitos suck
the blood up from their arms
because it isn't in their karmic interest
to inflict upon the vulnerable
unnecessary harm.

Mountain Lion

There have been rumors,
unconfirmed reports,
that you, long absent,
have returned.
The failed farms yielded
to the seedlings,
and the forests, first felled
centuries ago,
came back. It's not
the range historically
your line is used to,
but there's game
and people do not wander
too far off the trails.
There will be trouble
when you pounce
on someone's poodle.
More so on one of us.
The camera-phone, the modern-day
equivalent of the pitchfork,
will be brandished,
and you'll find returning
to the fringes difficult.
But there are those
who root for you
and understand you only know
predation, gliding
like an old fear through the woods
in which the civic-minded
will leave poison and take care
their hands do not get injured
setting the excruciating traps.

Bear Encounter

> "Identify yourself by talking calmly so the bear knows you
> are a human..."—National Park Service

The bear, I'm guessing, knows what century this is
and ambles like a luggage salesman from the fifties
up the gravel driveway to the back door of my home
because the worn path advertises that's the way
the people living here decided they would come and go.

The black bear does not knock because he knows I know
he saw me looking out the window by coincidence
as he came up the driveway, so there's no point
in pretending I'm not home, no point in flattening myself
against a wall behind a door until the bear,
deflated, feelings dented, finally turns away
and wonders what is wrong with me or, worse,
what's wrong and irremediable with him.

I therefore slide the door and ask, "How can I help you?"

"Your wife, she threw a pot at me this spring."

"I know. We had an argument about that."

"She home?"

"She's working."

"I was only eating birdseed. Didn't even bend the pole."

"I know. I'm sorry." I remove a square of suet
from its packaging and hand it to the bear.

He sits down in an Adirondack chair and says,
"Because I've been here plenty and I see her
watching what I'm up to from the window
and she doesn't seem to mind me being here."

I sit in the companion chair and say,
"She gave up nicotine this spring. Around then,

maybe later, she got on the Lexapro.
She microdoses now, so I don't know.
It doesn't curb her drinking like I read it might.
It's nothing personal to do with you
is what I'm saying. She's thrown pots at me."

"You understand all winter I live lightly, right?
I basically don't utilize a single natural resource.
All of it is yours as far as I'm concerned.
When I emerge come spring, though, hungry
as a motherfucker, I'd prefer your wife just say
'Hey, bear' or something civil if she doesn't want to share."

"Another suet?"

"Sure."

He thanks me when I hand it to him.
I sit down and ask where he picked up the language.

"Oh, you know, it can't be helped."

He eats his suet, and we listen to the birds.

I ask him what he knows about the myths
of man becoming bear and bear becoming man.

"That ship has sailed."

"What ship?"

"You have no spirit animal. No totem.
You don't have a clan."

"You want a beer to wash that down with?"

"In a bowl, if you don't mind."

We drink our beers in our own ways.
The sunlight filters through the maple.

"This is nice," he says.

"There's talk about a hunt, you know."

"Is that a threat?"

"Of course not. I just thought it's information
you should know. It's nothing imminent."

"You're angling for something."

"I'm just saying, if it comes to that, a hunt,
you have a safe space here."

"You're angling for something."

"No, I'm not. Like what?"

"Atonement."

"For the pot?"

"For everything," he says as he upends the empty bowl.

"Can I come with you?"

"You're not credible. You wouldn't last a day.
Besides, I can't get past this feeling
that you're hiding something from me."

"What if I were naked in the moonlight?"

"Naked in the moonlight," laughs the black bear,
disappearing through the trees and up the hillside
in the back. "You people."

On Not Shooting

"There is no such thing as the State
And no one exists alone;
Hunger allows no choice
To the citizen or the police;
We must love one another or die."
　　　　　　—W.H. Auden, "September 1, 1939"

The Greek word *xenia* means hospitality,
a code of welcoming the foreigner,
the person of another strain, another
homeland, into circumstances
that acknowledge similarity
in terms of wanting
to lave the grime of travel from our skin,
in terms of wanting in our stomachs
what replenishment the host can spare
and in our souls what company,
in terms of wanting to be on our way
with good directions in the light of day
and with the touch of parting.

Xenia also means the flow of pollen
from a plant strain to the tissue of another
plant strain's embryonic seed, no fear
of variation or hybridity,
no mechanism to prohibit
contact with the others.

A Generous Inaction

Question #28 is asking
in what ways have I enjoyed grace
from a stranger or a mere
acquaintance. Just so
we are on the same page,
instead of elegance of movement
I take grace to mean
what it's supposed to mean
in *There but for the grace*
of God go I, a jinx perhaps
if one considers that the man
reputed to have said a version of it first
while watching what the upright
used to make the English gallows do
was chained one morning to a stake
and burned beside a young man
who'd refused to say *Why not?*
and wink at his inquisitor when asked
if he believed the bread and wine
became in fact the body and the blood.

So in what ways have I enjoyed
unmerited benevolence
or favor that was of this world
and not of from a stranger or a mere
acquaintance is the question.

Yesterday a man in Washington
stood on a roadside by his lawn
and with his open hands
warned drivers of a line of deer
that crossed the road in dashes.
As happens now, a driver shot him
and confessed to the police
when he was found that in his mind

he feared those open hands
were coming for his life.

A month ago, I stopped short
on a shoulderless road
because a painted turtle wasn't fast enough.
I raised my index finger, gesturing
This won't take but a minute
to the driver stuck behind me,
never thinking that she could have
later claimed my springing from my truck
with such a finger was a provocation
that absolved her of preemption.
But she waited, and she waved and smiled
as I ran back to my truck,
my thumb up to express salvation,
which she also didn't shoot me for—
a generous inaction
I can't thank her for enough.

On the Seemingly Increasing Number of the Inhospitable in This Dimension

It has become so trying to believe
the person in your presence is a god
whom you subscribe to and is in disguise
to test your kindness toward the homeless
or to teach you something elementary
about the prophecies before he gives you
all the proof you'll ever need.

How comforting it must have been
to sit down with a stranger at your table
in Emmaus and be gobsmacked,
doubtless, right back to Jerusalem.

What if this evening you are old and poor
and vulnerable to a sensational demise
and two men of the peasantry, rejected
by your countrymen, knock softly on your door
and ask you and your partner
in this life if it is in your hearts
to spare for just this night some floor space
on which they might curl themselves to sleep?

If we're being honest, you'd deny them also,
offering a curt apology perhaps
but closing on them the impartial door,
considering the many ways that you are good
and rationalizing that such xenia,
if it was ever practiced,
isn't safe to practice now.

Let's say you are unusual
and let them in, allow them
to get clean, and feed them, pour them
wine that you were saving for yourselves

and notice each time you return to the carafe
that it's as full as ever, as it was
from the beginning. Would that be enough
to offer up your guard goose or your ancient dog
to these two whom the wine trick gave away?

When they reward your xenia by warning you
to get to higher ground before the flood, would you
tip off the others, giving them a chance, more time
to be a better version of themselves?
Or would you, as you watch them flail and gurgle,
say they had their chance already, fair and square,
and squandered it, which makes them people
it's okay to wash your hands of after all?

About This Business of Deserving

One day you realize that you've outlived
a lot of people, children, countless animals,
trees even, all of whom on that day seem
to have deserved duration more than you.

It's probably your birthday, so you just kick back
with a spirit of desired strength
and look up at the leaves or clouds
and try to listen to what they are saying
about this business of deserving.

Throat bared, comfortable, the pleasant
poison coursing through your bloodstream,
you are prone to make associations.

Maybe you recall the Thessalian king
who found out through a fortunate connection
to Apollo that the Fate
whose job it was to cut the thread of life
was on the verge of cutting his
unless the king could find a substitute.

He asked his parents, closer to the end
presumably than he, to take his place,
but they said life is just as precious
to the old and sent him on his way.

He asked his friends, associates, subordinates,
but all refused, all understood
that if your platelet count is dangerously low
perhaps it's just your body's way of saying
it is time for you to go, that if
your ticker is defective it's unfortunate
but there must be a reason
for the heart you were allotted, that if

you're hit by a speeding ox cart
while you're helping someone vulnerable
across the road it's just the luck of the draw
and if you're lucky the deserving
plays a featured role in what comes after.

Still, you can't help thinking
about the pair of American toads
run over in front of the tilted mailbox
in the thunderstorm last night
after how many hot days without a drop of rain.
How glorious the downpour must have felt
before the headlights bore down
like a dirty trick from a direction
that had just been perfectly dark.

Standing By

> "'Twas a sunflower-monkey on Neptune
> I imagined over the radio."
> —Allen Ginsberg, "Journal Night Thoughts"

My father used to stand with right hand half raised
and pretend to hold a pitchfork
like the male American in the painting,
drawling, "Spiders are our friends."

When I was too young to understand
that I could raise my voice in contradiction to abuse,
my cousin Richie, who was older by I think
three years, and someone else whom I've forgotten
used a pillowcase to gather frogs and toads one night
near the apartment complex where he lived
and brought them to the parking lot
where one by one they stomped on them
beneath the bug swirls in the sodium light
while I did nothing but shake my head
when Richie urged I take a turn.

When I was still too young, my cousin
Billy, older than me only by a year,
took me along when he went to a neighbor house
to water plants and take care of the dog.
We read the woman's finished quiz
in *Cosmopolitan*, and as we left he summoned
from some passage a Germanic loogie
that he spit with admirable precision
on the dog's spine and appeared to not have fallen
in the estimation of the dog.

When I was old enough, I tried to drink like Andre
Roussimoff, the Eighth Wonder of the World,
and had an image that I feared expressing

empathy for a bergall would probably have undermined,
so I said nothing as I sat back loaded in the boat
and watched as Ed, his mullet flapping in the sea breeze,
caught a few bergalls and played a game he called
bergall ball, lobbing each fish in the air
and batting it back out to the Sound
again and again as though a promising son
were in the outfield shagging flies.

Then one day not long after,
Ed was poaching lobsters, hand
over hand, a strenuous job and admirable
if you could separate the effort from the ethics.
I leaned back as usual astern, put down my beer,
and raised the cooler's long lid, watching lobsters poached
already process their captivity unbanded
and this second introduction of the light.
I lifted one and held him outside of the boat.
Ed said don't you let that fucking lobster go.
I let him go and reached in for another,
was assaulted, flipped without resistance
overboard for finally enacting a conviction
that would have to be enacted every day
how many times before the sunflower-monkey
comes to us for real this time, for good.

Aesthetics

Wherever there appeared a gleaming
slime trail from the night before
to make me think that something magical
had passed by the geraniums,
my father placed a saucer and then poured
cheap beer in it until it almost overflowed.

The story I was told was that the slugs
did not appreciate the beauty
of geraniums or other
ornamentals bordering the slab
of patio where we dined freely
in the summer and did not discuss
or even think about what the controlled
explosion of development had done
to the intricate biota.

I could not explain why I got out
of bed each night and tiptoed down
two flights of stairs and out the storm door
to upend the saucers, and my father
could not fathom where the beer had gone
when he picked up the saucers in the morning.

He's been rather dead
for more than twenty years, and still
I don't know if he hears me anymore
or sees what I've become.

I'd like to tell him
slugs have been hermaphrodites
for half a billion years.
I'd like to tell him that
last night while smoking an unmentionable
beneath a sugar maple that has been here

since the Revolutionary War
I turned my flashlight on and saw
two leopard slugs entwined
like a caduceus and descending
  slowly,
        slowly
  from a
        shining
  strand of
        mucus,
  spinning,
        spinning,
far more beautiful and stirring,
          I'm afraid to say,
than any patio geranium I've ever seen.

Anticipation

The hummingbird-migration map is telling me
the closest ruby-throated hummingbird's
in Newark, Delaware, two-hundred-forty miles or so
from here, about ten days away, eleven maybe,
fourteen-million, sixteen-million heartbeats distant,
give or take, but I suspend the spotless feeders
from their hooks this morning anyway
in case the unobserved are making better time.
It is the least that I can do for someone
who is flying all the way from Mexico
or Panama or Costa Rica, somewhere far
more tropical than here, to nest covertly,
bear young, perch, a burst of iridescence,
on this lilac tip that died three years ago,
and crane the green and ruby neck, uplift the eyes
and swordfish beak toward maple canopy, toward sky.
The etiquette of xenia, as I have known it
from the literature, does not apply.
We are not strangers. This is more their home
than mine, no matter what the papers say.
But there is reciprocity, exchange,
the spirit of equivalency. I'm tendered
something dearer than a four-to-one solution.
When the jewelweed is in bloom
and when the bee balm bobs
and when the sacred hearts of rhododendrons are revealed
and when the hummingbirds are on their endless sorties,
when they flutter on the branch tips
and tomato cages in the sunlight and the warm rain,
when for minutes at a time the hummingbirds become
parabolas above the cedars, when they hover
inches from my thankful face to reaffirm
an understanding, I forget
that I believe we're in that species of decline
that will be capitalized and duly noted
on the timeline of demises.

Gratitude

"It is my wish, then, that in every place
the men should pray, lifting up holy hands,
without anger or argument."—1 Timothy 2:8

If I'm being honest with myself,
I should be, when my time comes, gurgling
under the bituminous-seeming water
with the other sullen souls in Circle Five.

I've grumbled in the sun, the sweet air,
not about the sun and sweet air,
but I've grumbled, inwardly
I've grumbled when in general
and, now that I think about it,
even when I pick at the specifics
I should have been thanking someone
for the sunshine and the sweet air
and the circumstances and the genes.
The list is endless.

I sigh a lot.

Apparently it has been known
empirically for twenty years
that gratitude is good for you,
and all that time, when gratitude came up
as a professional-development motif,
I told myself that it was bullshit
and sent messages to that effect
to colleagues whom I trusted were as thankless.

When yesterday I learned that gratitude is so
salubrious, my first thought was how shitty
people were to practice gratitude
because it might boost serotonin

or talk hypertension from the ledge.
This is how the sullen think, I guess.
The other way I guess we think
is to imagine extrication
as impossible and to imagine there's no way
to truly will the frown into a smile.
This ain't like losing weight, we'll say,
or we'll quote Popeye.

But the thing that taught me maybe
I could shoot for Circle Two, the circle
of the lustful, maybe even Limbo
just above it, is a list
of a hundred questions meant to summon
gratitude into the sweet air and the light.

The first is easy:
What went well this week?
I thought about this and came up with,
well, my Texas heeler puppy found
a years-old pack of Trident
stewing underneath my seat
as I was heading down my driveway
toward a week in the woods in Maine.
I smacked the pack from his mouth.
My wife used hydrogen peroxide
to recall the sticks of gum.
Long story short, the puppy's fine.

The old me sighed and grumbled, rued
my negligence and then the world
in which a manufacturer of xylitol
is free to sell a canine poison
so close to the registers.

What may become the new me
thinks the puppy rubbing his back

against the deck boards, mottled forepaws reaching
toward the leaky porch roof
as though praising, thanking someone out there
for the gift of this imperfect day,
is onto something only four months after
he was tossed by a man from a window
onto a road in Tennessee.

Anecdote of Way Northeast of Tennessee

Tread lightly from this wooded wetland
by the rising discontinued road
the map shows
as an orderly progression
of parallel dashes leading from
a jar or two the wilderness
surrounds, which needn't mean
the wilderness believes the jar
or two are worth surrounding
or have alteration powers
other than what sedimentation
and gravity allow.

Walk a little
in the mud and find your footing thanks
to ledge and stones so old
they've been impressed
with faithful likenesses
of plants so old
humility sets in.

Watch out for the tawny
slugs whose kingdom this
has been for so long
there is not a fallen leaf they don't know,
not a decomposing trunk or stone
or mud slick they have not
with regal speed
and intimate adhesion
taken in, a tour
evincing no mismanagement,
no graft, no waste,
no hubris or preponderance
of self.

When the tentacles retract,
remember it is you
who are the source
of the retraction, the imbalance
in the kingdom, so again
tread lightly and apologize for being
the exclusive one, the only
one who's clothed and shod,
whose body is
at various removes
from earth and snooty.

The daughter of the dairy
farmer's black sheep
of a son lives in the new house
on the hilltop where the road
is uniform and tarred.
Ignore the stretch of junk
outside the fence that pens
her goats. Don't agonize
about what's leaking,
leaching from that sprawling pile,
heading for the kingdom
when it rains, how it's ingested,
passed on to the Class B
waterway below, to the Kenduskeag,
the Penobscot, and the bay.

Pretend to be admiring
the field of corn across the road
and know her father came
to town some months ago and tried
again to be a dairyman.
Know all he did was hang
surveyor's tapes on trees
that were not his and changed
the boundary of a poet's lot
below and was reported.

Know his mother tried to stop him
in a kitchen on the wood's edge
when he held the favorite
of his handguns to his head
and stared at her before the end.

Wonder did the wilderness rise up
to the casing on the floor
and sprawl around, no longer wild.
Let's agree the bullet took
dominion everywhere
some time ago, as overwhelming
as the chainsaw and the car.

But I am sitting at the bottom
of the discontinued road
and listening to the brook,
which doesn't sound impaired,
flow in a southerly direction.
Everywhere are seed deposits
and mosquitoes undeterred.
And here beside my wrinkled hand
this beetle rolling on.

Pardon

What I've learned since letting
the landscape I'm in charge of go
beyond what No Mow May prescribed
is that the vines are conscious
and have waited like who knows
how many generations of cicadas
for this string of days
in which no implement, no blade, no whirling
length of plastic string disturb
deep worship of the sun, a spring
and summer's worth of reaching
toward the fullness of assembly.

I've learned that if I let the wild
grapevines, tendril after tendril, climb
the whole way up the dignified American
red maple, they will spread and grow
fanatical and shade her, weigh her
down and stress her, kill her even
as the finches peck grapes
in the waning of my lifetime.

So I take my ersatz Crocs off
in defiance of my wife who claims that I
do nothing and walk past the staghorn
sumac kingdom, through the high
grass, stepping lightly, on
the lookout for amphibious
impressions, stopping underneath
the branch where contact first was made.

I hold between my fingertips
a tendril curled three times around
a branch tip and see tenderness instead
of strangulation, curiosity instead

of imposition. All the cultures
have a tale about a stairway, ladder,
vine, tree, tower, something that's the way
from earth to the divine, the other
side, the magical dimension
infinitely hovering above
our always ending own,
whatever you prefer
to call transcendence.

Tony Hoagland said, before
his pancreas was overwhelmed,
you have to decide what
you're willing to kill.
So I let go and touch the horseweed
and the bee balm on the way back
as I think about the pardoned
laboratory chimpanzee in puckered awe
as she looked at the unbarred blue sky
for the first time in her life.

Question #5

Gratitude-generation question #5
is what do I like about the chair
or table that I'm currently using.

I have sat on or reclined against
enough trunks and erratics in the woods
to know that I am grateful
for this cushioned chair and matching ottoman
who after all will wait here like Hachiko
on this floor long after it is obvious
that I am never coming home.

I get down on my knees and tip
the chair and then the ottoman to see
if there's a white tag that will tell me
something of their story, but there's only
stapled cambric, black, a void of sorts.

I sit back down, my feet up, held here
with no expectation that I'll take the chair
and ottoman to the woods one day and show them
part of the world that might remind them
of the one that they are from, North Carolina
bottomland swamp forest maybe, I don't know.

Seems an injustice not to know
at least the species of the tree they're from.

I get down on my knees again
to see what clues their legs might give me,
but I don't read wood grain well.
Could be oak. Or maple, cherry,
hickory, for all I know. And even so,
the frame's a deeper mystery.

I sit back down.

Most people wouldn't want to know
what came down with the tree,
whatever tree it was. But I do.
I imagine what was nesting
up there, what was living
unimpeachably beneath the bark.

Imagining such downfalls as I do
has strained my marriage more than once.
My wife does not get why I care.
She asks why can't the chair just be
a chair, why can't the ottoman just be
an ottoman, so I suppose that what I like
about the chair and ottoman
I'm currently using is,
besides their unconditional support,
the way they make me feel
unusual in that regard.

Cost of Living

Interest rates are rarely talked about
in poetry. The same goes for inflation.
Any economic benchmark really.
This makes sense to me. I'd rather read
a poem in which bats have made a comeback
and are dining on mosquitoes
as the summer night takes over, dotted
as it used to be by fireflies.
But I'm not living in a world
where bats are on the rebound from a syndrome
or where fireflies are numerous enough
that no good parent, lounging
on a patio in darkness, sees a problem
with allowing kids to bottle them for fun.
I'm living in a world
where Cyndi Lauper's seventy-one
and where, as bad as things have gotten
in Khartoum, a place of astronomical
inflation, they are nowhere
near as bad, our envoy says,
as the trajectory suggests they'll get.
I trust the envoy. I remember
sending money after seeing a fly
on the forehead of an Ethiopian boy
too weak to shoo the fly away.
I don't believe I've seen a video imploring
money and compassion for Khartoum.
I'm searching. It is sad
that where the White Nile and the Blue
converge lived river hippos once,
and once there was a hippo goddess
worshiped by the ancients as a fierce
protector of the unborn and the young,
and once the Yellow Nile wasn't
just a wadi in the desert to the west.

Question #9

It felt like a lifestyle choice,
the purchase of this graceful
piece of molded plastic
that sat so low in the lake
I lived by at the time
that I believed I suddenly acquired
the perspective of the ducks.

It was good for me, the floating
on an element so at the mercy
of what entered roughshod from the land.

But then I moved
eight miles away,
although I fully understood
the lake would stay right where it was.

I had to drive now
1.7 miles with the kayak
bungee-corded in the bed
to put it in the tidal river.

It was not the same.
I put the kayak in
a lofty shed and left it
there with mice for years,
a terrible ingratitude, I see now.

Having read that gratitude is something
you can practice, I've been practicing
by answering each day a question
from the gratitude-generation list
and, if it's feasible, enacting somehow
for enhancement what I answer,
sort of like Ben Franklin,

though he tried to practice thirteen virtues
whereas I am only staring down the one.

The question is
*What hobby or activity
has made you truly happy?*

I take the kayak down and drive twelve miles
to the landing of a quiet
tributary of the tidal river
and discover I am grateful
for the uneventful getting in
and for the gliding underneath
the two-lane bridge that leads in one direction
to the opera house where I've sat
with my mother at a musical
before the onrush of dementia.

I forgot
that there are modest houses here tucked in
the woods like residential secrets
that my kayak and the tributary
tell me, and I'm grateful for the gifts
of confidence and access but I also think
that it would be ideal
to live in secrecy like that
and have a greater cause for gratitude
than someone gliding by. Thanks
to my kayak and the tributary,
this ungrateful notion passes,
slowly first and then at once
because a long-jawed orb weaver
in the middle of a web
with give, strung taut
between the lowest overhanging branches
of a maple leaning toward the tributary,
pins me with its eyes because it knows

that what I am is capable of worse.
A mother and her ducklings know this also
and are seamless as they paddle
to the farthest bank from me.
I do not get as close as I intended
to the plaque beside the dam and fishway
where the water churns and flows
in the direction of the landing.

I forget which is the color
of the foam that is organic
matter decomposing harmlessly
and which the color of the agitated
chemicals they say will last forever.

I'm happy, truly, that the ducks and I
are paddling parallel courses
at a mirrored pace,
and I am grateful that from bank
to bank the tributary, even after
all the rain, is just this wide.

Consensus

"All the rivers run into the sea,
Yet the sea is not full;
To the place from which the rivers come,
There they return again."—Ecclesiastes 1:7

Go down this road. Or any road
around here. You'll see
five-inch by five-inch yellow squares
on top of tilted stems where grass
is on the verge of yielding
to the humdrum terrors of the road.

I steal these, box them up, and mail them
to the companies that left them.
I have excellent penmanship
and put inside each box a note:
a quote from Swedenborg and my opinion
that a livelihood of broadcasting
neurotoxins, coating trees and bushes,
flowers, soil, insects, everything
that keeps this house of cards together,
can't be how the company people really
want to show the love they must feel for the world.

A young policeman shows up
at my house, and I explain myself.
I promise nothing but assure him
I am no John Brown, no Ted
Kaczynski, which produces
a pronounced change in his brow.
I tell him I am *no* John Brown, *no*
Ted Kaczynski, but my shift in emphasis
just furrows him more deeply
and makes more peremptory his tone
when he says leave the little signs alone.

I'm here to tell you books still make a difference.
If I never read a word
that Edward Abbey wrote, I doubt
I'd have these little confrontations,
these ubiquitous conflicts I believe
the right words deputized me to resolve
or deputized me to at least make known in these parts
that among us walk the sort who think
they hear the voiceless and are trying
in the spirit of apology and xenia
to say back something hopeful, welcoming.

I look around and wonder
how I might do something
on the order of unfurling
the crack down the monstrosity
that's still Glen Canyon Dam.
The Colorado's dying, though,
so maybe it makes sense to wonder
how I might do something more.

They've put red dye in the Connecticut,
a mile down the road from here,
and think they can anticipate
how herbicide will flow next year
and take out only the hydrilla.
I can tell you now how this will go:
the way it always goes.
I have a year but no idea
how to convince who needs convincing
that too much official faith
has been placed in dispersion
and it couldn't hurt to ask
what the alluvium and sedge and freshwater
mussels have in mind or how the small fry
and the dabbling ducks would like to see
the Army Corps of Engineers proceed.

In Theory

"We treat the attrition of lives on the road
like the attrition of lives in war. Horrifying,
unavoidable, justified." —Barry Lopez, "Apologia"

More than anything else I'll have to answer for,
the nine odometers that logged the miles
I have put on Earth will show whoever's judging me
that countless good intentions I have hosted
like a lazy seedsman never had a chance.
Convenience was a sort of fallen angel
whose recruits had gotten to me long before
I had the faculties to fathom what there was
in me originally that could be gotten to.

When people ask me if I'd kill the baby
Hitler, I reply I'm fairly confident
I would and ask them if they'd kill the baby
Karl Benz or the baby Henry Ford, and when they say
they wouldn't, no, I ask them would they strangle
the Sumerian baby who would otherwise grow up
six-thousand years ago and lay the first baked bricks
to expedite the plague of human restlessness, would they
drown the baby who would otherwise grow up
and lay the world's first stretch of asphalt road,
and when they ask me who did that and I say
that his name eludes me but I'm certain
he was Belgian, they say no, anonymous
or not, Sumerian or not, they wouldn't kill
a baby fated to accomplish something they declare
I must admit was bound to happen anyway.

What Might Have Been

It's no one's fault, and even if it were
it happened long enough ago,
a time when we still practiced taking cover
under desks we all knew were unable to prevent
the vaporization of our elementary selves
if finally the endless posturing ended
and we entered Armageddon
with our fingers laced behind our tucked heads
and our knees pressed to the tiles
no one ever told us were primarily asbestos.

Mrs. Hansen, ancient then but younger
as I see her from my fifties, passed out
the occupational-prediction test
and sat back down behind her ruling province
of a desk, the thin-gauge chain
that shimmied from her eyeglass temples
stilling as she estimated maybe,
row by row, how we, the sniffling,
cowlicked lot it was her fate that year
to oversee, might fare in life at thirty.

I won't say that the test results inspired me
to take up smoking for a while, but they did
suggest that playing baseball for a living
didn't seem a reasonable prediction
if the questions really had elicited from me
the answers that unveiled my natural
inborn aptitudes, which I believed
they probably had. It was like looking
in the mirror after an abiding feature
of my face had been removed or rearranged,
and that was how I had to see myself,
to think about myself, from there on out
because it was the way the world would.

It didn't make me want to start a Reich
or anything like that, but it was something,
pivoting like that before the end of grade school
and believing I was made for business management
or politics when it turns out that I was not.

I wish the test had not been so much
an elicitor and simply told me, knowing
how impressionable I still was then,
exactly what the plants and animals would need
from me when I became employable, exactly
what the air and soil would require of me, what the water,
simply fessed up that my aptitudes
were actually approved conspirators
against what it turns out I hold most dear.

Not Exactly Dubbed

I've reached that stage of life
where I've accepted I will not be dubbed.
I won't be asked to bend the ceremonial knee.
I'll never feel the light touch of a sword
upon my shoulder or my bowed head,
wherever the sword's required to alight
to consummate the transfer of nobility.
Does this stage make me sadder
than my entry into late-stage middle age?
We're taught to dream beyond our early station,
so, provisionally, I must say yes,
but after all the time I've spent with birds
and squirrels, red and gray, and chipmunks
and the world of insects and arachnids
I must say, this poem notwithstanding,
that I rarely care that there will never
on my answering machine or in my mailbox be
an invitation to a castle to be dubbed.
And that's okay. It really is.
Just yesterday, my legs extended in the sun,
a dragonfly alighted on my big toe, fixed me
with its eye bulbs, nodded, and went still
while we enjoyed the warmth and light together.
Just this morning, on my shin, a titmouse
landed sideways, cocked her tufted head, and rode
a wave around the shingled house.
And just now a red squirrel scrabbled up
my chairback, perched upon my shoulder
for a minute, maybe less, and left me feeling
not exactly dubbed but statuesque,
like Lincoln staring at the obelisk across the way.

Starting Point

> "A tree's a tree. How many trees do you need to see?"
> —Ronald Reagan, candidate for governor
> of California, March 1966

Where do I begin?

Let's start on the Avenue
of the Giants. I confess
I've never been, but I believe
I can imagine. What I can't
imagine is a Californian
born and raised
in Illinois proclaiming
two months into his first term
as governor, "I saw them.
There is nothing
beautiful about them, just that
they are a little higher
than the others." I am only
marginally ashamed
to say that more than once
I've welled up in the presence
of a low tree's beauty
and expect I'd fall
apart beneath the redwood's.

What candidate Reagan
actually asked the Western
Wood Products Association in that
friendly banquet hall in March
of '66 was slightly different
from this poem's epigraph,
which is the misquote
commonly reported: "I mean,
if you looked at a hundred-thousand

acres or so of trees—you know,
a tree is a tree,
how many more do you need
to look at?" Reagan's audience
responded with the ambient chuckle
he'd expected and were not awaiting
a specific number since they knew
that in their world there was none
but were happy with their candidate's
polite fuck you to those
who had in mind a ballpark figure
and had no faith Reagan's gaze
was wired to appreciate the value
of a forest, temperate-rain or otherwise,
except in terms of board feet.

Which reminds me that my mother's
mother had dementia
and would always comment on the height
of trees, the only thing about them,
I suppose, that she had registered,
that had remained.
And that reminds me
that my mother has dementia
and is always looking upward
at the eldest trees and asking,
"If that big tree there comes down now,
who's responsible because
when it comes down you better watch it,"
as though nothing else about a tree
that's been around since Washington
or Lincoln warrants a remark
except its height and its demise.

I follow Julia
Butterfly Hill on Facebook, meaning
that I'm counting on a tenuous

affiliation to absolve me
of the work of actually inhabiting
a threatened tree (not necessarily
a thousand-year-old redwood) for a time
(not necessarily two years,
eight days) that's long enough
to do some stubborn good.

It doesn't even need to be about
inhabiting a tree as long
as it's about confronting
comforts we've been taught
we are entitled to and bringing
to some portion of the world's
attention the attendant harms
of carrying on as usual.

Sometimes I take back what I have said
about there being nothing worse,
no action less effectual
than writing poetry to counteract
the exponential depredations.

There's a meme in circulation
in which on the left six corporate logos
are arranged and on the right
six leaves of common trees,
an illustration that
identifying and identifying with
what's on the left are easier,
more natural than with what feels
on the right like venerable irrelevancies
or relatives we never cared to know.

Can we start over?
Let's start there.

Leaving the Oldest Tree in Maine Alone

The map of what's been cut
from here clear up to Maine
since the incursions
shows that almost all
of the originals and everything
within and on them
shuddered and were rudely
taken, rudely told
their squatting days were over.

Mr. Doyen used to sip his clear booze
in a clear glass, poring
over maps of places
he would never see in person.
I'd stand by his armchair, asking
what this cartographic feature was
or that, intending to appear
like someone who would not be
smoking weed so deeply
in his son's Camaro minutes hence.

The ways we should and should not be
successors to the fathers
are negotiated somehow
by a spirit in an ice cave.

After overdoing it one night
as an advanced adult,
I woke and drove northwest
to Goshen, where a black gum
has been living mostly incognito
for the last six-hundred years.
I hiked in to the swampland,
and I saw there was no way
I'd find the old-growth tupelo

without some serious guidance
and was happy for the failure.

In the spirit of the Widow Douglas,
I took snuff
and drove to Massachusetts
where the oldest tree is in a forest
under state protection
and accessible to such as me.
I sat beneath the eastern hemlock
who was born around the time
of Shakespeare's mother,
and I wondered if such context
was another species of diminishment.
I camped that night nearby
the hemlock, and I don't remember
fretting over lifespans
or mysterious allotments.

I fasted on the third day
and apologized to nature
for the fumes that trailed me
up to Buel's Gore, where I shut the car off
at a trailhead and had visions
of the eastern hemlock that has lived
the last five-hundred years
below the Camel's Hump
on which I stood two hours later, clueless
as to who the eldest was or why
my torso tingled so.

The next day I replenished
my electrolytes but otherwise
ingested nothing but an eighth
of mushrooms on my way east
to New Hampshire and the black gum
who has lived there since

we'll call it 1323, three centuries
before New Hampshire ever was.
I found the road that ended
well shy of the wetlands,
and I wondered who I was
to think it was okay
to try and get a handle on longevity
and loss by serially invading
what should be inviolate.

I parked two car lengths
from a brand-new Cherokee that idled,
and I couldn't say if I had heard
an outcry ever for the model's name change.
I decided I would look
at black gums from afar,
without interior narration,
but I saw the woman slumped
against the steering wheel,
her brown hair lustrous, widespread
down her back, no scarring
of a tree ring in the black gums,
no contraction to record her passing
at the age of twenty-nine.

Accidents of Birth

Turns out the Book of Matthew doesn't say
which magus brought the myrrh,
which got me thinking what the hell
is myrrh. Apparently a myrrh tree
birthed Adonis right out of the trunk
and bark, no afterbirth, no cord,
if you believe the oil paintings
of the Renaissance and after,
just a beautiful baby with a family
history the tabloids would have loved.

Modern Love

If we were hospitable enough
to let two bums in for the night
and it turned out the bums were gods
from a mythology I never felt
the visceral sectarian fervor for,
I'd have to ask my wife for confirmation
of the bums' miraculous replenishing
of the wine in the carafe we use for company
because, if it turned out that I forgot
I was the one who kept refilling it,
she'd never let me live down
my spontaneous conversion,
one more sign the cognitive impairment
that's bedeviled women on my mother's side
for generations finally branched out.

But if she looked me in the eyes, unusual
because what we so often practice is aversion,
then I'd know that I was sane and would be with her
on a high point when the flood came, watching
suffering on such a scale that we would wonder
if the moral thing to do was leave the high point.
But we wouldn't leave. We'd wait,
adjusting to the status of the chosen,
as the flood, receding, showed us more and more
of what would dry out and be ours.

In the midst of watershed events,
adrenaline or something flows and people say things
it's impossible to walk back once they're said.
If we were still communicating
with the gods and she requested of them
to allow us when the time came
to expire simultaneously, I would,
because I know what happens next

and finally to Baucis and Philemon, interject
and ask the gods instead to not transform us
into trees around here since we know
the human population will rebound and limb
or prune us to make way for roads and wires
or clear us out entirely to keep us
from the water lines and leach fields
of the new development.
I'd kneel if necessary, praying
that they'd somehow send us when the time came
to a remote grove just below the tree line
on a mountain in the West and turn us
into bristlecone pines in reasonable proximity
so that four-thousand years from then or even five
we still might be around to wave hello.

State of Nature

—for Andrew Sheldon

Since it turns out, Shelly said, that most of us
don't really mind or even notice being
poisoned by non-ionizing radiation
and whatever the ingredients of chemtrails are,
God's in no rush to intervene,
which, if it's true, the lagging intervention,
seems to me a massive violation
of the contract God and I agreed to
through a lifetime of observances and rituals
that go back to the old days,
days of covenants and testaments
and sometimes visitations of destruction
on a scale incomprehensible to all
except the righteous or the lucky
left behind to try again.

Perhaps the evidence of mutual love
was never widespread. Maybe the contractual
you scratch my back and I'll scratch yours
has always been a tilted fiction
servicing a charismatic goon.
Maybe everything we need and love
is lying dormant in an untold story
that enough of us must listen to and passionately tell
enough times that the other stories,
those that sprinkle our destruction,
those that rake in billions,
finally become expressions
of an unrelatable morality,
like God persuading Abraham
that it was time to kill his son.

Imagining the End

Some days I'm with Hobbes
and don't desire life without the State.

The folks who hunt for pleasure
would exhaust their prey in no time,
and I'd feel an obligation
to prevent them, skipping
an appeal to reason altogether
and proceeding straight to force.
The reputation I'd develop
as an interspecies empath or a soul
who yearns for regulation
would require me to further spare
a portion of my freedom
and devote more time and mental energy
than average to alertness
and approaches from behind.

I tell myself I might not mind reverting
to a time when it was wise
to drink small beer instead of water,
but as soon as I start dreaming of relaxing
in the long light of a summer's evening
with a farmhouse ale beside a dappled somewhere,
quite pleased to have made it through
another day alive and unmolested,
Hobbes reminds me someone's always bound,
if not this evening or tomorrow
then a day not far beyond, to try
and commandeer my water source,
to beat me senseless for my grain,
to seemingly befriend me
and then stab me with a crude knife in the back
as soon as I let down my guard
and share my fermentation secrets.
Yesterday, however, Ursula K. Le Guin

reminded me that there were many, many
crowned and sceptered days when it appeared
impossible that an alternative
could actualize, evaporating
the divine right of the kings and queens
who are exactly what now.
Whoever said imagining the end
of the world is easier than imagining
a functional alternative
to capitalism was as bound
as I have been by other
than a natural law, by other
than a power absolutely irresistible.

I know that where I'm sitting now
is not a jungle in Colombia,
that there are forces there
that are not here, where I'm alone
in woods and elbowed out by no one,
though I am unarmed, as vulnerable
as any animal who might be taken in
or out of season underneath the very noses
of the people overseeing animal security.

By 2060, the prediction goes,
the human population of the world
will start to fall as quickly as it rose.
I'm hoping we are like the animals
who pause their pregnancies
in times of scarcity or stress.
I'm really hoping, though I won't be here,
that one by one what precious newborns do come
come to understand how they can keep
the numbers workable, how scale
is critical, proportion, balance,
how they can with song or story
put behind them the residual desire
to commodify it all.

Petition

Three years my senior, Bob Bartley used to say
he played each varsity football game
as though it were his last. I didn't ask
if he'd foreseen a ligament detaching, snapping
like a rubber band one Saturday afternoon,
or if that statement was his way of mentally preparing
for a starker showdown with finality,
which probably it wasn't, but he did die young.

Myself, I thought too much and always left
at least a little something in the tank
in case I needed it the next day for an undertaking
better suited to the picture I was forming of myself.

I quit the team in tenth grade, drifting
from the fungal locker room, relieved
that one less system would be bugging me
to merge with something larger than myself,
to give my all this year and probably the next
before I saw the abnegation
and the hard work paying off, returning
to me that allotment of my ego
that was finally allowed to bask in adulation,
which I did and didn't want in measures
that this late in middle age I still cannot explain.

I can't explain why this late in the game
I think of Bob as often as I do.

It may just be that I have memorized
that scene in *Hamlet* in which Hamlet is amazed
at how the unsung soldiers who have no shot
at the big time do not hesitate to die for nothing
more than honor in the hinterland.
It may just be that Bob's resemblance
to the first Van Halen frontman is enough

to trip in me the light fandango of nostalgia.
It may be that I can't help remembering
how Bob's transmission failed him
so that he could only drive his Monte Carlo
in reverse, which for a week or so he did
without an accident or being stopped by the police.
It may be that how Bob passed on in beautiful weather
in the Sound has stuck with me,
and probably, since I'm still living each day
like there's plenty more where this one came from,
what I'd like to know, if you can hear me, Bob,
is if you lived the last one like it really was
your last and if, in your opinion, after all
these years, that makes a difference in the end.

Idyll

In 1976, a sparkler flaring
in each hand in celebration
of the Fourth, I couldn't have
imagined that Estonia
or any other country in the world
could be more free than what the song
has always said quite clearly
is the land, no irony,
no winking, of the free.

But there it is.

The Human Freedom Index doesn't lie.
I've checked it fifty times, and each time
Latvia is still four places higher
than America, which I was taught
was basically a synonym
for freedom. We are tied
for seventeenth with Lithuania
and the United Kingdom. Countries
I had no idea were countries,
no offense to Cabo Verde,
are as close to us in terms of being
free as we are to New Zealand,
poised at number two, this close
to Switzerland, the leader
of the free world, which I can't help
feeling should be our position, #1,
the perch and title we would have
to jump the likes of Luxembourg
and Denmark to reclaim.

If you had told me all this
on the Bicentennial, I would have twirled
my sparklers in your eyes

and found my father by the orb grill
or my grandpa who had ties to World War II
and asked if it could ever be true
that a country that has never been
the setting of a Western
or the home of Abner Doubleday
could ever be more free than we are.

We'd listen to the sizzle
of the flesh whose plight was not on us
and to the independent fireworks
on other blocks, in other yards,
to ice cubes and the opening
and closing of the Coleman,
to unbridled laughter and to talk
of mostly nothing, to mature
forsythia adjusting to the breeze,
and we'd know that no other country
in the world was waiting as we were
for nightfall and the big show to begin.

Rut

The older I get, the more I can't refute
the evidence that we're susceptible
to ruts, some deep, some shallow, on some level
threatening to keep us locked in
to an undesirable trajectory
despite our innocence of any crime.

I've finished lunch, a tuna dollop
on a salad bed, and now am standing
on a gym mat in a high-school weight room.
It takes several minutes to prepare the mind
for pull-ups, which I do on Tuesdays.
This is Wednesday, though. Memorial Day
was Monday and will ripple through the week.

Descending on the final pull-up of the set,
I see how the routine will be unusual
if I combine it with my poetry routine,
a strictly weekend practice. So I write
what you have read. What more is there to say?

I do set two and walk around the weight room,
reading scotch-taped messages of inspiration:

Doesn't Matter. Get Better.

In order to perform in front of thousands,
you must work in front of no one.

What have you done today to beat Bunnell?

I do set three and lean
against a load-bearing column painted
black and white, school colors.
I look around for something else to tell you.

On a white board by the door,
the bench-press leaders are immortalized
in dry-erase marker: *315, 275, 265, 240, 225.*
I think of how my muscles have become
progressively less massive.
I'd give anything
to cling to a respectable plateau.

I pull as hard as ever on the fourth set
and return to leaning on the column.
On the wall beside the squat rack,
next to a cutout of the wrestling coach's face,
a square of paper tells us who
the bench-press leaders were in 2010:
345, 335, 325, 320, 300, 290.

I look back at the bench-press leaders of today.
I don't see progress. I don't see that
the inspirational messages have gotten through.
I worry this might be a sign
of where we are now as a country.
On the other hand, the Appalachians
may once have been as high or even higher
than the Himalayas are today.
So maybe we are simply in the process
of becoming lesser mountains.

Either way, I dedicate my fifth set
to the word *plateau.*
I grunt *plat* on the way up,
teau as I go down, again
and again and again, until I know
I can't hold on a second longer.

Drifting from the Faith

The black cross that a thumb smudged
on my forehead on a Wednesday
drew stares in the world but no derision,
no suggestion of uncleanness.
It told everyone I'd made a vow
to give a dear thing up for forty days
because I didn't think I'd make it
that long in the desert on my own.
I wouldn't have objected to an eye roll
here and there. The text is adamant
about not practicing your piety
in order to be seen, and what's a black cross
smack dab in the middle of your forehead
but a plea for one's attention as you pass?
The season and the ritual keep me
coming back each year, the weirdness
of the marking and the going forth
as though I were the poor goat
on whose head the annual accumulation
of the village's impurities and sins
was put, the goat who smelled
the blood and burnt flesh of the offerings
as he was led out to the desert, left there,
separate from the village nonsense,
wondering in goat terms what now.

Breaking with Tradition

The world abounds in marvels.
But you knew that, and you know
that knowing isn't witnessing.
When you knock softly on the hive three times
and whisper news of someone's death
and drape the hive in black, you know
that anything could be happening inside
the hive but you choose to believe
that grief has bloomed inside the hive
and you are glad that the tradition
doesn't mandate verification,
doesn't ask you to produce a single bee
in mourning and you're glad
because it's wonderful to just believe.
But I don't have a hive. I have a lawn
I haven't mowed in going on three years
and I have bees of different species
lolling on the goldenrod and jewelweed
in the sunlight gracing all of us
like one creation on this afternoon.
I lean in to a sprig of goldenrod
and to a bumblebee I whisper,
"Brother Ryan died today."
The bee appears unfazed, untouched
by grief, appears to have no plans
to fly the bad news to the hive.
It may be that the work must come before
the grief can be indulged because
the season doesn't last forever after all.
The sun is on my neck. I bend down
to the honeybee inside the jewelweed,
child of the sun, and once again I whisper,
"Brother Ryan died today."
The bee backs out and hovers, level
with my eyes, then level with my lips, a honed

intelligence who seems to know what I'm about.
The bee flies off to jewelweed and to jewelweed
and to jewelweed, and the sun is high,
and I am telling you it feels wrong
to expect a bee, who, if she's lucky,
has about two months to live, to care
about the passing of a man who had been
in the world since 1948. It is enough
to say the words in sunlight, waist-high
in the goldenrod and jewelweed, to release them
one more time among the most bees
I have ever seen, forgetting that today
the daylight will be more or less
two minutes shorter than it stretched out
yesterday and more or less two minutes
more than it will be tomorrow.

Inflammation

In my memory, I'm younger than I know I was.
The truth is I was nineteen on the eleventh
of September, 1987. I was nineteen
on the twelfth, the day I sat down
at the table in my parents' house and read
that Peter Tosh was shot dead in his home
on the eleventh at the age of forty-two.

I write this now because last night I read
in *Boulevard* about a person born
with poliomyelitis, which I hadn't known
was one of the myelitises and which reminded me
of Peter Tosh because each morning
in the shower I do what I can
to back him up on "Reggae-Mylitis,"
which begins, "Woke up this morning
With a funny, funny feeling,"
and proceeds to put an optimistic spin
on a condition that traditionally inflames
the spinal cord, disrupting
the brain's responses to the body.

Peter sings of the progression
of afflicted parts, from bone to blood
to toes to brain, but doesn't sound afraid
of giving up control and doesn't sound resentful
that the doctor answers none of his concerns.
He simply tells us how this category
of myelitis moves without impediment
through his body, a connecting thread
like in the song about the foot bone's
connection to the leg bone and the leg bone's
connection to the knee bone
except the neck bone is the terminal connection
in that song whereas in "Reggae-Mylitis"

there's holistic interplay. His brain
is touched. His temperature is high.
His soul's on fire, and his mind has been
subsumed before whatever's going on
comes through his mouth and into his fingers,
doubling back to register in his brain,
reminding him again that he has been inflamed,
and every morning Peter Tosh, long gone,
reminds me of what happened on the day
of Pentecost when tongues of fire landed
like myelitises on the apostles
and an ancient barrier was suddenly removed.

Free Association

When my father came home
from his father's funeral,
he said we might be Russian,
Jewish even. He said other things,
like how his father looked
better than he had in fifteen years.
I still don't know if that was humor
in the process of transmuting grief.
My mother didn't want me
seeing death at that age.
I was eleven, old enough
to say goodbye, to wrestle
with the undefeated. What she was
thinking I can't say, but even now
I rarely go to funerals. I'm smiling
now because I'm thinking, probably
because of what my father said
in line four, of the palest person
I have ever known. Michael Rosen,
known as Spider, shielded
by the highest-number sunscreen,
was the first to take a *Playboy*
from his father's bureau
and reveal it to us in the daylight
with a play-by-play narration
of its glossy contents.
He and I were sitting at a table
in a tony place in Georgetown
overlooking the Potomac River
on a June night in the Clinton years.
Spider was more confident
and buzzed than I had ever seen him,
and he leaned back in his chair
and said with borrowed smoothness,
"Hey, now," each time someone lovely passed.

It is the world's way sometimes
not to recognize an inborn gentleness
as the default. So I explained
that people didn't know him
well enough to laugh. They didn't know
the number sunscreen he depended on,
his inability to tie a tie.
I don't remember when I saw him last,
but I remember in that era he was dating
someone domineering from Iran
and I was working for a man named Lovejoy,
caring for two Shelties
named for isles in the Hebrides.

Isn't It Romantic?

I've tried to walk in woods like Wordsworth
did with Dorothy, his sister and stenographer,
but no one will accompany me
with pen and paper so I go, a goon, alone.
A different time, a different place, a space age
of inventions stretching from their sooty time
to the particulates afloat in mine.
I do the same thing with Thoreau, my weirdo
hero: moon, idealize, say progress
isn't what it's been cracked up to be,
and tell whomever I am drinking with
the wheel, the light bulb, and the particle
accelerator ruined everything.
But even if you advocate clean coal
and do not mind the disappearance
of the mountaintops and the impossible
logistics of containing slurry;
even if you champion the push
to try our hand at going nuclear again
and do not fear the half-life;
even if you seriously believe
we can invent or innovate our way
around catastrophe and end times,
surely there is something we have left behind
that even you would not deny
you sometimes dream on your commute
of getting back to in a perfect world.

Eighty-Sixed

Disasters like the burning Amazon
are visible from space, no magnification
necessary, if you have the wherewithal
to launch yourself and orbit, gazing out
the window, one hand cradling a cheek
and portion of your mandible in mellow awe
as you observe the smoke whose drift
is imperceptible and feel a twinge
because you know your planet had it all.

From space, unmagnified, the skeletal boy
in Gaza, dead now anyway, is nothing
to your naked eye, but you can see
the imprint of destruction and determine
as your breath condenses on the outer reaches
of your palm if it is worth it to be this
detached when there is so much down there
aching for another voice, another hand.

In 1966 the ultimate founder
of the *Whole Earth Catalog* was tripping
on a roof in San Francisco and believed
if NASA loosened up and let us see
the satellite photo of the whole Earth
it would alter human consciousness.
How could it not?
How could it not change for the better
our relationship to Earth and to each being
trying gamely not to die?
But if that change is true, if it occurred,
I'd hate to think where we would be today
without the image on the cover of the *Catalog*
that first day of September, 1968.
Inside, the Purpose's first sentence read,
"We are as gods and might as well get good at it."

On Christmas Eve that year, Apollo 8
was orbiting the moon. Bill Anders snapped
the famous Earthrise photograph in color
and believed, as Stewart Brand had,
that the image of our Earth out there alone
and marbled white and blue was something
capable of turning the foreseeable disaster
into something closer to the way it was
before the demarcations and the falls.

Bill Anders, in an interview on the 50th
anniversary of the photograph,
said it's really too bad we're still shooting
at each other on this tiny little place
that we call home. I wished
I could have asked him if he thought we are
as gods and, if so, if he thought we are
about as good at it as we would ever get.
He did say somewhere, I discovered later,
that from his perspective God gave us the stage
for our performance. How the play turns out
is up to us, which sounds like something God would say
before the waters or the horsemen come,
like something someone who has read *Macbeth*
behind a bar he's tended for too long might say
before he wipes his hands and turns the light out
on the one place that for all these years would have us
and that by some miracle took this long
to conclude our kind is welcome here no more.

Moving On

I have no friends now who will hold me
upside down and pour beer up my throat
while I cling to the keg rim for dear life.

No one in my life now counts the seconds
I can keep it going, guzzling from the tap,
defying gravity in some respects, and losing
brain cells in the name of nothing
but an undistinguished bacchanal.

Some who used to be so integral
to my upending moved to one or other
of the Carolinas or to Florida.
Some others stayed and opt for mixed drinks
as they socialize with people who hold
similar views on children and lacrosse.

Myself, I moved a major water body
to the north away and learned that friendship
is a habit that requires cultivation
and routine, a shared geography
or interest, something vital that coheres
because a history and past
affection weaken slowly otherwise.

You may be thinking I am just a boomer
who aspires to the pathos
of the lonely Anglo Saxon in the elegies
that record the turmoil after loss
of gold-lord, mead hall, kinsmen,
and you may be thinking I have fallen
far short of the aspiration.

This is not an elegy, however.
I may be a boomer, but I don't aspire

to inversion with abandon anymore.
The years have taught me that I left
because my birthplace had no mountain
or expanse of forest that accorded
with the standard I was born with.
The years have taught me that I left
because I could not think among my old friends
that an insect is as worthy of its life
as I am of my own, and likely more so.

But I miss them, which is not to say
I want them back. Surrounded by a pine
and hemlock forest, sheltered by a porch roof
from a dense June rain, I listen
to a hermit thrush and miss them.

Vastness and the Theme of Inescapability

The sort of beer I drink is better
in a shapely glass, although a sainted brewer
in Vermont vows the experience
of drinking his creations is enhanced
if they go down directly from the can.

The man became a millionaire
by following his bliss, which means
he knows whereof he speaks,
but I prefer to separate my beer
as soon as possible from BPA,
the endocrine-disrupting chemical
that lines the can's mysterious interior.

You may point out that BPA's ubiquity
is proof of harmlessness or proof
that we are powerless against the vastness.

I would not confess this normally,
but I am not as horny as I used to be
and I suspect that BPA —
the studies back me up on this —
may well have flimflammed my testosterone
and burgled my charisma.

You may say that BPA has leached already
by the time the beer goes in the glass.
I will not argue with you there.

You may be thinking why don't I just drink
my beer from green or brown glass bottles, which I do
from time to time, but you have seen
the cool shelves and the outcome
of the packaging decisions
and concluded that aluminum is in.

This brings us back to the unsettling
acknowledgment of vastness and the theme
of inescapability. The probable
carcinogen glyphosate is in
the bottled beer the same
as in the canned and is no friend
of my testosterone, and PFAs are likewise
in there, probable genetic fiddlers,
and prepared to do unnatural things
to the organic regulations
that have gotten all of us this far.

I know you're thinking
why don't I stop drinking.
That's been on the table for a while.

I'm open to the possibility
that I can't shake, subconsciously, the need
to handle shapeliness and put it
to my lips without negotiation
whenever I desire.

But when I'm sitting as I am now
in this cushioned Adirondack chair, sipping
a local eight-percenter from a tulip
glass as I observe a mother
sparrow teaching her buoyant young
to pick and eat the peppergrass seeds
that loll above the paver seams
my wife sprayed with an herbicide
about ten years ago, I really need
the sparrows and the peppergrass
and all the others, can or no can,
to on some transparent level know
that I know we're in this mess together.

Reversion

The apprehension of the littleness of individuals,
the feeling little, humans mostly cope with
in the basic ways. A certain strain
of human battles littleness, denies it, via acquisition
of material, of money, of position, of facility
with the guitar or saxophone, of progeny, of flesh,
of alcohol or cannabis or LSD or ecstasy or oxy or whatever,
of unrivaled medical care, of knowledge, gnosis,
of a parakeet or hamster—anything
that argues you are bigger than the person with the tiny house,
the person with no car, the person with no managed wealth,
the person whose employment is dependent on the broom,
the person whose interior has never felt the groove,
the person who will not live on through offspring cells,
the person whose charisma's insufficient
to recalibrate the intercourse parameters,
the person who's afraid of nectars and elixirs
and expansions and has never seen the Dead,
the person with no doctor or with no hope
of a private room, the person who has died,
the person who has never seen the light,
the person who does not repose before a parakeet encaged
and thank a god for liberty, the person who does not repose
before a hamster on a fixed wheel and reflect
on calories and energy expenditure and going nowhere.
There is more.
A certain strain of human, facing the immensity,
embraces littleness, takes refuge in it, wishes
the embracing and the refuge-taking could be of
a purer quality, the purity of an American toad
residing temporarily beneath the moss, appendages
and belly practically the earth, its inner self synonymous
with solitude and biding and subsistence,
letting practically the whole of this existence be
except when circumstance and hunger whip

the sticky tongue out and a smaller life goes down.
And even then, its appetite so limited, it is no slave to appetite.
It is a bare-bones synthesizer
of available nutrition, an ascetic, no marauder,
no obsessive, no philosopher of death, no epicure.
Beneath the green moss, an American toad may be
a better Buddha than the Buddha, and the moss
perhaps a better Bodhi tree. The humans
of this strain envision bare necessity and picture
living in the manner of a toad or water bug
or any being independent of the toothbrush
and the power and the key and the dimensional lumber
and the wardrobe and the mattress and the coffee
and the box and the delivery and the insistence
on a certain quantity of happiness
and the experiment and the advance and the and the and the.
And some of them, to supplement envisioning,
conduct computer research on the extant peoples
who are still one with the old ways—
the Sentinelese, the Korowai, the Old Believers, and the other
tribalism keepers—and discover that they envy them
their isolation and simplicity and tiny carbon footprint
and holistic vibe. They envision freedom from amenity,
encumbrance. They discover also the internal
recognition that reversion, biological reversion,
is, in essence, requisite if they expect to really strip
things down, go backward, generation after generation,
say goodbye to the refrigerators and the televisions
and the various music-delivery systems they have known
and the Colecovisions and the gums, the xylitol,
and the disease preventatives, the fortifiers, and the books,
the bulbs, the spectacles, the arch supports, the mops,
the lollipops, the dildos, everything their distant forebears
did not have a need for or a concept of. Goodbye. Goodbye.
And they discover that divestiture is more
than just the giving up the goods. There is the longing,
the allegiance to the circumstances

into which, sans consultation, they were born,
the magnetism of habituation, the awareness of the pose
they would be striking when they make believe
they do not know what's out there or ahead,
when they pretend there's nothing naturally internalized
and nurtured that they miss. And so the full commitments
to reversion are remarkable, are few.
Holding an ideal and thinking of yourself as capable
of being its embodiment and then deciding,
after multiple evaluations, that the full-commitment ranks
are so thin, so rarefied that shame or quitting status
probably will not accrue to you if the totality of the ideal,
the scope of abnegation and activity required,
cows you into rationalizing
that the sensible thing to do is to adopt
a principle or two of the ideal and practice
with artisanal intensity what henceforth
you take satisfaction in considering to be your life's work—
that is the commitment route
most people who identify with littleness
and anonymity and treading lightly settle on.
The specter of that settlement does not abandon them.
It is a species of regret, like knowing
that you said you would defend a weakling
and then stood in the vicinity, observing leaf veins,
rapt in vascularity, as he was beaten.
You have questions in the aftermath.
It's difficult to argue your proximity was something.
You do not forget the beaten weakling
or your standing by, and you believe
more clearly in the narrow dedication than you ever have.

About the Author

John Popielaski is the author of the novel, *The Hollow Middle* (Unsolicited Press), as well as several poetry collections, including *Isn't It Romantic?* (Texas Review Press). His poetry has appeared in a number of journals, including most recently *Bicoastal Review*, *Canary*, *Common Ground Review*, and *Public School Poetry*. His second novel, *Attuning*, is forthcoming from Broken Tribe Press in late 2025, and he has recently been promoted to the status of a person by whom a house wren at long last has consented to be hand fed.

Sheila-Na-Gig Editions